TRUE OR FALSE?

This person can make the dead tell secrets. →

TRUE!

Dead bodies aren't great at conversation. But they often have important secrets to tell. Forensic pathologists find those secrets. They examine dead bodies in murder cases and other suspicious deaths.

It's not a pretty job. Bodies arrive with ID tags on their toes. Pathologists look inside their stomachs. They check under fingernails. They poke at livers and kidneys. They test body fluids.

If they're lucky, they find out how, why, and when a person died. Secrets like that can help put a murderer in jail.

Book design: Red Herring Design/NYC

Library of Congress Cataloging-in-Publication Data
Joyce, Jaime, 1971–
Toe tagged : true stories from the morgue / by Jaime Joyce.
p. cm. — (24/7: science behind the scenes)
Includes bibliographical references and index.
ISBN-13: 978-0-531-12067-5 (lib. bdg.)   978-0-531-18735-7 (pbk.)
ISBN-10: 0-531-12067-8 (lib. bdg.)   0-531-18735-7 (pbk.)
1. Forensic pathology—Juvenile literature. 2. Forensic
pathology—Case studies—Juvenile literature. 3. Medical examiners
(Law)—Juvenile literature. I. Title.
RA1063.4.J69 2006
614'.1—dc22   2006005875

TOE TAGGED

True Stories From the Morgue

Jaime Joyce

WARNING: This book involves real-life murder cases. Some of the cases may be disturbing—like the ones that involve cutting open dead bodies. And that would be all of them!

Franklin Watts®
A Division of Scholastic Inc.
New York • Toronto • London • Auckland • Sydney
Mexico City • New Delhi • Hong Kong
Danbury, Connecticut

3

CONTENTS

FORENSIC 411

Before you bury yourself in the rest of the book, find out what forensic pathologists really do.

8
OVERHEARD AT THE CRIME SCENE
To the Morgue!

10
SEE FOR YOURSELF
Dead Man Talking

12
WHO'S WHO?
The Forensic Team

These cases are 100% real. Find out how forensic pathologists solved two murder mysteries.

15

Case #1:
Murder in Philly

A young woman drowns in the bathtub. Is it an accident? Or is it murder? Can a forensic autopsy help investigators solve the mystery?

A young woman is found dead in a Philadelphia suburb.

29

Case #2:
Rush to Judgment

Forensic experts go to great lengths to prove a man's innocence.

Was a woman pushed down some stairs in Shelburne, Nova Scotia?

FORENSIC DOWNLOAD

Examine this! Here's even more amazing stuff about forensic pathology.

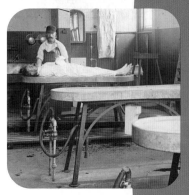

44 FLASHBACK
Key Dates in Forensic Pathology

RIPPED FROM THE HEADLINES **46**
In the News

48 REAL STUFF
Autopsy 101
Autopsy Tool Box **50**

52 CAREERS
Help Wanted: Forensic Pathologist

YELLOW PAGES

56 RESOURCES

59 DICTIONARY

62 INDEX

64 AUTHOR'S NOTE

Every murderer leaves behind one important clue: the victim's body.

FORENSIC 411

It's a forensic pathologist's job to find the evidence. When did the victim die? What caused the death? Was there foul play? The answers to these questions lie beneath the skin—and under the fingernails and in the blood.

IN THIS SECTION:

▶ how FORENSIC PATHOLOGISTS really talk;

▶ what they look for on a DEAD BODY;

▶ whom they work with at the CRIME SCENE.

To the Morgue!

Forensic pathologists have their own way of speaking. Find out what their vocabulary means.

"Did someone call the medical examiner? We need a doctor here at the crime scene."

medical examiner
(MED-uh-kul eg-ZAM-uh-nur) a doctor who directs the examination of bodies in murder cases and other suspicious deaths; also called *ME*

homicide
(HOM-uh-side) murder; the killing of one human being by another

"I may not be an expert, but I think we're dealing with a homicide. How accidental can ten stab wounds be?"

morgue
(morg) a place where dead bodies are examined and stored

autopsy
(AW-top-see) a complete examination of a dead body. An autopsy is done to determine how and when a person has died.

"Let's get the body back to the morgue for an autopsy."

The Greek word "autopsia" means "to see with one's own eyes."

8

Say What?

"Call in a forensic pathologist. We're going to need a specialist's help."

forensic pathologist (fuh-REN-zick path-OHL-uh-jist) a doctor who examines dead bodies for evidence to be used in court

"Patho" means "disease, suffering." "Ologist" means "someone who studies."

"Let me know when the forensic autopsy results are in. I want to know if I have the evidence to arrest this guy."

forensic autopsy (fuh-REN-zick AW-top-see) the examination of a body for evidence in a court case

Here's some other lingo a forensic pathologist might use on the job.

clinical autopsy (KLIN-uh-kul AW-top-see) an autopsy done on someone who has died of natural causes
"You've got the wrong lab. This is the crime lab. We don't handle **clinical autopsies.***"*

coroner (KOR-uh-ner) an elected official who investigates sudden and unnatural deaths
"Call the **coroner.** *There's no hope for this guy."*

exhume (eg-ZOOM) to dig up a dead body
"I wish they had done an autopsy before the burial. Now we have to **exhume** *him."*

foul play (fowl play) an act or instance of criminal violence
"This case was no accident. It feels like **foul play** *to me."*

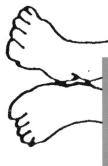

Are there any broken bones? That could indicate foul play.

Are the **victim**'s nails broken? That could mean that there was a struggle. And skin or blood found under nails can be tested to see if it matches a **suspect**.

Are there cuts, bruises, or scrapes on the skin? Pathologists study them for clues. The size of a stab wound, for example, could relate to the size of the killer's knife.

Urine from the bladder is taken to test for drugs.

Dead Man Talking

Every dead body has a story to tell. It takes a forensic pathologist to make sure its voice is heard.

A body is found and no one knows why the person died. Was it murder? Suicide? A strange hidden illness? In cases like these, police call in a forensic **pathologist**. The pathologist performs an autopsy to answer three questions.

The kidneys and liver are examined to see if the victim was beaten. Pathologists also test these organs for poison.

Air passages might show traces of soot from a fire or water from a drowning.

Does the body have tattoos or birthmarks? These marks can help police identify the body.

c

Is there food in the stomach? Is it fully digested? The answers can help determine time of death.

Tiny red marks in the whites of the eyes could be a sign that the person was strangled.

Plastic bags are placed over the hands until the autopsy so that **evidence** won't be lost.

1. What is the manner of death? This question has five possible answers. The manner of death could be natural, accidental, homicide, suicide, or undetermined.

2. What is the cause of death? Cause of death is more specific than manner of death. It has to do with exactly how the person died. For example, in a homicide the cause of death could be a gunshot wound, stabbing, poisoning—or something else.

3. When did the person die? The answer can help catch a suspect in a lie. (See Case #1.)

How does the body help answer these questions? Take a look at the diagram above, and you'll see. (Then, if you still have the stomach for it, turn to page 48 for a step-by-step guide to an autopsy.)

The Forensic Team

Forensic pathologists work as part of a team. Here's a look at some of the experts who help solve crimes.

FORENSIC NURSES
They help with autopsies. They collect, preserve, and document evidence found on the body.

FORENSIC PATHOLOGISTS
They examine bodies for clues in murder cases and other suspicious deaths.

DETECTIVES OR AGENTS
They direct the crime investigation. They collect information about the crime, interview witnesses, identify suspects—and arrest them if there's enough evidence!

DIENERS
They work in morgues and help with autopsies. They weigh and measure bodies. They also help to confirm a dead person's identity.

FORENSIC TOXICOLOGISTS
They're called in to test victims for drugs, alcohol, and/or poison.

MEDICAL EXAMINERS
They're medical doctors who investigate suspicious deaths. They try to find out when and how someone died. They often direct other members of the team.

TRUE-LIFE

CASE FILES!

24 hours a day, 7 days a week, 365 days a year, forensic pathologists are solving mysteries.

IN THIS SECTION:

▶ a woman falls in the shower. Was it an ACCIDENT OR MURDER?

▶ another woman falls down a flight of stairs. Was it an ACCIDENT OR MURDER?

Here's how forensic pathologists get the job done.

What does it take to solve a crime? Good forensic pathologists don't just make guesses. They're scientists. They follow a step-by-step process.

As you read the case studies, you can follow along with them. Keep an eye out for the icons below. They'll clue you in to each step along the way.

 THE QUESTION At the beginning of a case, pathologists identify **one or two main questions** they have to answer.

 THE EVIDENCE The next step is to **gather and analyze evidence**. What was the person's medical history? What can be observed on the body? Pathologists study the answers to find out what they mean.

 THE CONCLUSION Along the way, they come up with theories to explain how, when, and why a person died. They test these theories against the medical evidence. Does the evidence back up the theory? **If so, they've reached a conclusion.** And chances are, they've come up with evidence that could help crack the case.

Merion, Pennsylvania
April 30, 1997
12:39 A.M.

Murder in Philly

A young woman drowns in the bathtub.
Is it an accident? Or is it murder? Can
a forensic autopsy help investigators
solve the mystery?

Death in the Bathtub

Police get a panicked 911 call. Craig Rabinowitz says his wife has drowned in the bath.

Stefanie Rabinowitz seemed to have it all. She had a successful law career. She lived in a wealthy suburb of Philadelphia. She had a loving husband and a beautiful one-year-old daughter.

Then, at age 29, it all came to an end in a terrible accident. Or so it seemed.

Craig Rabinowitz made the call in the early morning hours of April 30, 1997. A 911 operator answered the phone. Craig sounded panicked. His wife was in the bathtub, he said. She wasn't moving and he couldn't wake her up.

Stefanie Rabinowitz was just 29 years old when she died in her own bathtub.

Police arrived within minutes. Craig showed them upstairs to the bathroom. There, still in the tub, lay Stefanie's lifeless body. She wore a watch, a ring, and some other jewelry. Medical technicians tried to revive her. But Stefanie was already dead.

Stefanie Rabinowitz lived in Merion, Pennsylvania, a suburb of Philadelphia. She was just 29 years old—a successful lawyer, a wife, and a mom. On April 30, 1997, her husband found her dead in the bath. How did she die?

The police wondered, What could have caused her sudden death? Craig had been home watching TV, he said. He found his wife dead in the bath around midnight. Could someone have sneaked in and killed Stefanie? Police searched the home for signs of forced entry. No windows were open. All the doors were locked. Had Stefanie Rabinowitz simply drowned? Did she slip and hit her head in the bathtub? To police, that seemed like the best explanation.

Stefanie's body was removed from the home. It was taken to Halbert Fillinger, the Montgomery County coroner. Fillinger would decide whether an autopsy was needed.

By the time medical technicians arrived, Stefanie Rabinowitz was dead. Her body was taken to the coroner's office.

WHO'S IN CHARGE HERE?

Coroners? Medical examiners? Forensic pathologists? What's the difference?

L ike many smaller communities, Montgomery County didn't have its own medical examiner. The coroner had to send Stefanie Rabinowitz's body to Philadelphia for an autopsy. Here's who does what.

Coroners are usually elected or appointed. In most states, and in some parts of Canada, they do not have to be doctors. They sign death certificates. They generally do not perform autopsies.

Medical examiners are required to be doctors. In some states they need training in forensic pathology as well.

Forensic pathologists are doctors who are specially trained to investigate cases of sudden, violent, and unexpected death.

The Husband's Story

Detectives bring Craig Rabinowitz in for questioning.

Craig Rabinowitz, Stefanie's husband, claimed he was watching TV just before he found his wife, dead.

The next day, Craig Rabinowitz met with detectives. He arrived at the Lower Merion Township police station at 6 P.M. Two officers questioned him for about an hour. They wanted to know exactly what happened the night Stefanie died.

Craig recalled the entire night for the detectives. He and Stefanie had eaten at a Chinese restaurant. They got home at around 7:30, he said. Then he took their daughter, Haley, for a walk. He and Haley were back by 8:00.

At 11 P.M., Craig said, he was in the bedroom, watching a hockey game on TV. Stefanie was in the bathroom. She was getting ready for bed. At around 11:45, Craig heard a thump.

"I had heard it a thousand times," he said. "It was when the shampoo falls off the holder."

"How much time was there from the thump until you went in and found Stefanie?" the detectives asked.

"Thirty-five minutes," Craig said.

Craig told the two detectives that he tried to pull Stefanie from the tub. "I don't know why, I just couldn't get her out," he said.

Just before Craig left, detectives asked him a final question. Did he have life insurance on his wife? Craig

According to Craig Rabinowitz, it was 11.45 P.M. when he heard a noise from the bathroom.

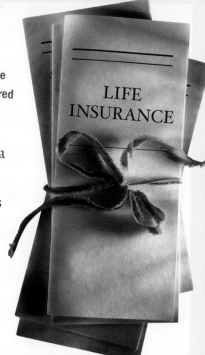

Craig Rabinowitz had a life insurance policy on his wife. Detectives wondered if he killed her to collect this money.

said yes. He could collect more than a million dollars after Stefanie's death.

Could Craig have murdered his wife for the money?

The detectives needed more information about Craig. They also needed an autopsy report.

Signs of Struggle

Does Stefanie Rabinowitz's body hold clues to the mystery of her death?

Halbert Fillinger didn't need to know about the life insurance. As coroner, he was in charge of Stefanie Rabinowitz's body. And he was already suspicious. Stefanie was young. She was healthy. No one had witnessed her death. To Fillinger, it didn't sound like an accident. He ordered an autopsy. Stefanie's funeral would have to wait.

Dr. Ian Hood, Philadelphia's deputy medical examiner, or **ME**, performed the autopsy. He knew that police initially thought Stefanie's death was an accident. He also knew that Fillinger thought it might be murder. As a forensic pathologist, Dr. Hood knew how to tell the difference.

What was the manner and cause of death? Hood was determined to find out.

The doctor began the autopsy with an external exam. He looked for bruises, cuts, and other marks on Stefanie's body.

It didn't take long to find evidence of a struggle. Around Stefanie's neck, Hood discovered some scrapes. The skin had been rubbed away. He also found tiny red marks on the inside of Stefanie's eyelids.

Next, Hood began the internal exam. He found undigested food in Stefanie's stomach. The food was still recognizable. Hood decided it was shrimp and bean sprouts.

So far, the clues pointed toward homicide. But Hood needed more evidence. He ordered a **toxicology** test to see if Stefanie had drugs in her system when she died. When the results came in, he would make his report.

[Forensic Fact]
Tissue samples are usually stored for 3–5 years after a forensic autopsy. In cases of suspicious death they can be stored longer.

DRUG TEST

Experts can find signs of poison in a body long after death.

In every autopsy, experts test the body for drugs or poisons. The tests are done in a toxicology lab. Toxicologists can test tissue from an organ, blood, and urine.

Pathologists usually collect a sample during the autopsy. They send the sample to the lab for testing.

The toxicologist tries to determine three things: What kind of drug was used, if any? How was it taken (through the mouth, a needle, etc.)? When was it taken? The answers help an ME or pathologist decide how and when a person died.

The Body Talks

What did Dr. Hood learn from the autopsy?

Hood considered the evidence. The marks on Stefanie's neck looked like they had been made by human hands. The tiny red spots on the eyelids were **hemorrhages**. A hemorrhage is caused when a blood vessel bursts inside the body. Strangling tends to burst blood vessels in the eyes of the victim.

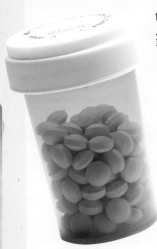

Tests showed that Stefanie Rabinowitz had a big dose of sleeping pills in her system when she died.

The food helped Hood place the time of death. Food stays in the stomach for about three hours after it's eaten. After that, it moves into the small intestine. Craig Rabinowitz said that Stephanie and he finished eating well before 7:30 that night. If so, Stefanie must have died before 10:30. Craig said he heard the thump at 11:45 P.M.

When the toxicology results came in, Hood had everything he needed. The tests showed traces of a sleeping pill called Ambien in Stefanie's blood. She had twice the normal dose in her system.

The results were clear: Stefanie's death was not accidental. Dr. Hood ruled her death a homicide. The cause of death was "manual strangulation." Stefanie's killer had choked her with his own hands.

[Forensic Fact]
Homicide is the sixth-leading cause of death in the United States. Ten percent of deaths in the U.S. each year are the result of homicide.

Busted!

With the autopsy report in hand, police close in on Craig Rabinowitz.

Stefanie's autopsy results came as a shock to her family. Craig insisted he was innocent. But police felt sure he had killed his wife. On May 5, 1997, they arrested Craig Rabinowitz and charged him with murder. His daughter, Haley, went to live with Stefanie's mother. Less than a week had passed since his wife's death.

With Craig Rabinowitz under arrest, police searched the suspect's home. They found business records and receipts. The papers showed that Rabinowitz was deeply in debt. They also looked at phone records. They discovered that he was involved with another woman.

As police dug further, the evidence piled up. Craig Rabinowitz had bought the life insurance policy on his wife just a few months earlier. Police also checked pharmacy records. Craig had a prescription for Ambien. That's the powerful sleeping pill that was found in

When police searched the Rabinowitz home, they discovered financial records. The couple was deeply in debt.

Stefanie's body. Rabinowitz had bought a new bottle of pills the day before Stefanie died.

By the fall, lawyers for the county were ready to go to court.

Case Closed

Craig goes to trial—then to prison for life.

On October 30, 1997, Craig Rabinowitz appeared in court. He was charged with murdering his wife. Everyone was ready for a long and difficult trial.

But Rabinowitz ended the trial before it began. He told the court that he had recently had a dream. In the dream, he was in the house he grew up in. Three dead loved ones were there: his father, his father-in-law, and his wife. The three said to him, "Craig, it's time to do what's right."

Rabinowitz decided to follow the advice. He admitted to killing his wife. He had drugged Stefanie. While she slept, he choked her with his bare hands. Then he put her in the tub to make it look like she had drowned. He did it to get the insurance money so he could pay off his debts.

The judge sentenced Craig to life in prison. Rabinowitz was led from the courtroom. Before he left, he tried to explain what he had done. "I lost the ability to know right from wrong," he confessed. **24/7**

Craig Rabinowitz appeared in court on October 30, 1997. He was accused of murdering his wife, and during his trial, he confessed to the crime. He was sentenced to life in prison.

DR. AUTOPSY

Dr. Michael Baden has performed more than 20,000 autopsies.

You may know him as the guy on the HBO series *Autopsy*. But important government agencies like the Federal Bureau of Investigation (FBI) know him as the guy to call to find out how someone died.

Dr. Baden has been a medical examiner for more than 45 years. Now, in addition to hosting his TV show, Dr. Baden is a forensic pathologist for the New York State Police. "If someone dies in jail or custody or on the highway," Baden told crimelibrary.com, "I'm available to explain what happened."

Old Mysteries

Dr. Baden also uses new forensic techniques to investigate old mysteries. In the 1990s, he examined the body of slain civil rights leader Medgar Evers. Baden found evidence that led to the conviction of Evers's murderer.

Baden was also involved in examining remains that may have belonged to the last royal family in Russia, the Romanovs. The Romanovs were shot in 1918. Baden traveled to Russia to identify their remains in 1992.

A Career in Autopsies

Like all forensic pathologists, Dr. Baden went to medical school. But he points out that there are many jobs in forensic science that don't require a medical degree. He advises young people, "You should inquire of your local police departments as to their standards for employment."

For Dr. Baden, this kind of work is extremely rewarding. There are very few forensic pathologists in the country, he explains. If he didn't do this work, it may not get done. He told crimelibrary.com, "Most satisfying to me is being able to explain to family members what happened to their loved one."

In this case, a woman died in suspicious circumstances —and her husband turned out to be the murderer. In the next case, another woman dies in a mysterious accident. Will her husband, too, prove to be the killer?

Rush to Judgment

Shelburne, Nova Scotia,
Canada
February 20, 1989

**Forensic experts go to
great lengths to prove
a man's innocence.**

A Fatal Fall

A woman tumbles down a flight of stairs and dies at the hospital.

At first, it looked like a terrible accident. On February 20, 1989, Janice Johnson lay at the bottom of her basement steps. Blood spread out slowly around her. She was barely conscious. She struggled for air.

It was 7:51 A.M. in the small town of Shelburne, Nova Scotia. Janice's neighbor, Robert Molloy, had just arrived to drop off his daughter. Janice was supposed to babysit. Her husband, Clayton, and their two daughters had already left for the day.

Janice Johnson was rushed to the hospital after she was discovered at the bottom of a flight of stairs.

When Molloy saw Janice, he ran to call for an ambulance. Medical workers arrived within minutes. They tried desperately to save the bleeding woman. She was rushed to the hospital, barely alive.

At 8:11 A.M., Clayton Johnson arrived at the school where he taught industrial arts. A secretary told him to get to the hospital right away. He arrived just before his wife died.

Clayton Johnson spent 15 minutes alone with his wife's body. Then he helped police piece together what had happened.

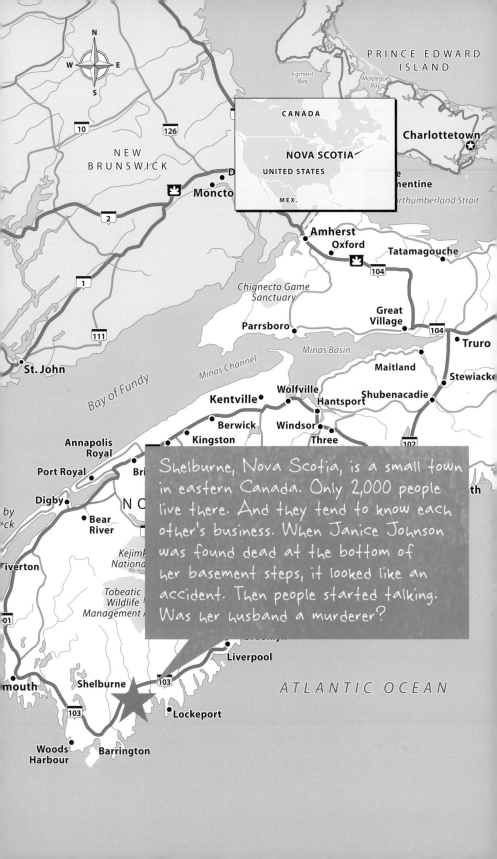

Shelburne, Nova Scotia, is a small town in eastern Canada. Only 2,000 people live there. And they tend to know each other's business. When Janice Johnson was found dead at the bottom of her basement steps, it looked like an accident. Then people started talking. Was her husband a murderer?

Clayton Johnson insisted that he had nothing to do with his wife's death.

At 7 A.M., Clayton Johnson had called Molloy. He asked Molloy to bring his daughter over at 8:00.

At 7:40, Clayton watched his two daughters get on the school bus. He left for work a few minutes later. When he kissed his wife good-bye, she was on the phone with a friend. Her brother was supposed to visit any minute. And Robert Molloy would be there soon.

Then Janice Johnson must have fallen down the steps. The accident happened between about 7:45 and 7:51 in the morning.

But was Clayton Johnson telling the truth?

Open and Shut Case

Clayton Johnson's story is confirmed by witnesses— and the body of his wife.

Police checked out Clayton Johnson's story. They talked to the friend who called Janice Johnson that morning. She said she heard Clayton's voice over the phone. He said, "See you later, hon." Then she heard a kissing sound. That was about 7:45 A.M.

Police also talked to other people around town. Several friends had seen Clayton Johnson driving to work that morning. He stopped for gas. He drove slowly behind a school bus for several miles. He made the 16-mile (26-km) trip by 8:11. Police figured he must have left by 7:45. His wife's phone conversation ended shortly after. Malloy arrived at 7:51.

How could Clayton possibly have murdered his wife? He had only three or four minutes to kill her, hide the weapon, clean himself up, and leave for work. He knew people would be arriving soon. Why would he choose that morning to do it?

Roland Perry didn't think Clayton Johnson was a murderer. Perry was the chief coroner of Nova Scotia. He performed the autopsy on Janice Johnson. He didn't see any signs of a struggle. There were no bruises on her hands or arms.

Perry decided that Janice Johnson had died from a severe head injury. Her skull had been crushed. The right side of

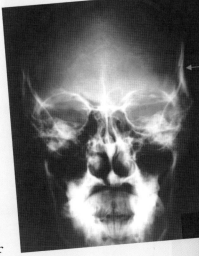

Janice Johnson's skull had been crushed in an accidental fall. That's what had killed her, coroner Roland Perry decided.

An officer from the Royal Canadian Mounted Police reenacts what Coroner Perry thought happened to Janice Johnson. First, she fell down the stairs, and her head landed in a gap.

her head showed a deep wound. The other side had smaller scrapes.

Perry studied photos of the Johnson home. The position of the body was hard to explain. Janice lay on her back at the bottom of the stairs. One leg rested on the bottom step. Had she turned in midair as she fell?

It wasn't a perfect explanation. But everything else pointed to an accidental death. The bloodstains were around her body. If Janice Johnson had been beaten, blood would have spattered on the walls.

Perry also noticed a five-inch (13-cm) gap between the stairs and the basement wall. He concluded that Janice Johnson had been a victim of terrible luck. She slipped on something at the top of the steps. When she fell, her head landed in the gap. The force crushed her skull.

Then, according to Coroner Perry, Janice Johnson's body flipped around. She landed on the floor, facing up. Later, some people would point out that this theory seemed very unlikely.

Coroner Perry filled out a **death certificate** for Janice Johnson. He said the death was an accident.

Clayton Johnson was left to care for his daughters in peace.

Questioning the Coroner

A new investigation puts Clayton Johnson in the spotlight.

On one point, everyone agreed: Clayton Johnson had suffered a terrible loss. But as the seasons changed, so did public opinion.

Three months after his wife's death, Johnson began dating again. His new girlfriend, Tina Weybret, was 22. Johnson was 52.

People in town began to talk. It was too soon for Johnson to start dating, they thought. In a year, the couple was married. Had their relationship started before Janice's death?

Before long, a police corporal named Brian Oldford overheard the gossip. He started to investigate. Had Tina Weybret been a **motive** for murder?

Oldford also learned Clayton had $125,000 in life insurance on his wife. Clayton had bought the policy just months before she died. But Oldford overlooked an important fact. At that time, teachers in Nova Scotia were offered a new insurance plan. Almost *half* of them bought a new policy at that time!

Oldford then found two women who had helped clean the basement after Janice Johnson's death. He showed them photos of their friend's body. Suddenly, the women recalled seeing blood spattered on the walls of the basement. They had said nothing about the stains when they first talked to police.

Oldford called in two forensic pathologists, Charles Hutton and David King. He shared the new information with them. The men discussed the story about the blood **spatters**. They came up with a theory. There had probably been a struggle. Someone had hit Janice Johnson on the head. The murder weapon was probably a baseball bat or a wooden board, they said.

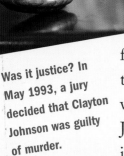

Was it justice? In May 1993, a jury decided that Clayton Johnson was guilty of murder.

Oldford gave his new findings to Coroner Perry. Perry decided to change Janice Johnson's death certificate. He said her death was a homicide—a murder!

In April 1992, police arrested Clayton Johnson. He went to trial for first-degree murder. The judge warned the **jury** that the case against Johnson was weak. But on May 4, 1993, the jurors found Johnson guilty. He was sentenced to 25 years in prison.

FOR THE RECORD
Every death has paperwork to go with it.

Everyone gets a certificate at birth. It lists all the important details: your name; your parents' names; and when and where you were born.

A similar thing happens when you die. A death certificate lists the date and time of a person's death. It also lists the manner and cause of death.

When a hospital patient dies, the hospital tells the coroner or medical examiner. The coroner or medical examiner issues the death certificate. If the cause of death is not clear, it's the coroner's or ME's job to order an autopsy.

In this case, the coroner, Roland Perry, performed the first autopsy on Janice Johnson.

Seeking Justice
From behind bars, Clayton Johnson reaches out for help.

Clayton Johnson tried to appeal his case twice. He was turned down both times. In 1995, he got some help. A group called the Association in Defense of the Wrongly Convicted agreed to investigate his case.

Lawyers James Lockyer and Phil Campbell worked for free. They set out to prove that Johnson was innocent. Their most important evidence would come from several pathologists. One of them was Dr. Linda Norton, who works in Dallas, Texas.

THE QUESTION
Could Dr. Norton figure out once and for all how Janice Johnson died?

THE EVIDENCE
Norton examined all the evidence. She looked at photographs of the Johnson home and of Janice's body. She read the police report, hospital records, and Perry's autopsy report.

After considering the facts, Dr. Norton agreed with Dr. Perry. Janice Johnson's death had been an accident. But Dr. Norton did not agree with Dr. Perry's theory about *how* Janice had fallen.

THE CONCLUSION
"I think I was in the shower when it hit me," Dr. Norton recalls. "Wait a minute," she thought. "Suppose Janice fell backward?" This would explain the position of the body at the bottom of the stairs. It would also explain a bruise on the back of Johnson's leg.

Lockyer and Campbell wanted to test Norton's theory. They contacted Dr. Herb MacDonell. MacDonell is a blood spatter **expert**. He runs the Laboratory of Forensic Science in Corning, New York.

MacDonell set up an experiment. He found space in a high school near his home. On the school stage, he built a stairway just like the one in the Johnson home. He then hired a young model named Heather Murphy to re-create the fall. Murphy was the same height and weight as Janice Johnson.

Murphy strapped on a safety harness. Then she let herself "fall" down the stairs. Dr. MacDonell had marked sections of the stairs with blue chalk. The chalk rubbed off on Murphy's body where she touched the stairs and wall.

This test proved that Norton's theory could be right. A backward fall could have produced the wounds on Janice Johnson's body. MacDonell wrote up a report. "I find nothing that suggests a beating of any kind occurred in the Johnson home," he said.

Lockyer and Campbell decided that they had enough evidence to get Johnson out of jail. In March 1998, they turned over their research to the Canadian minister of justice. They asked that Johnson be given a new trial.

A SAFE LANDING

Here's how Herb MacDonell proved that Janice Johnson could have fallen backward.

Herb MacDonell wanted to test Dr. Linda Norton's theory that Janice Johnson could have fallen backward. But how could he do that without hurting someone?

MacDonell got an idea when he read about a local production of the play *Peter Pan*. In the play, actors were hooked up to a safety harness so they could appear to fly over the stage. MacDonell asked one of the actors, Heather Murphy, if she would take part in his test—using a safety harness. Murphy immediately agreed to help. These pictures are from a video of the test.

The stairway was just like the one in the Johnsons' home. And Heather Murphy was the same height and weight as Janice Johnson.

During the test, Murphy was attached to a safety harness. And Herb MacDonell (*left*) was careful that her head didn't strike the stairs.

Though it's not clear from these photos, MacDonell had marked the stairs with chalk. That way, he could see what parts of Murphy's body struck the stairs.

The test proved that Janice Johnson could have fallen backward and had the kind of injuries that were found in the autopsy. (Note the safety harness.)

Free at Last

Clayton Johnson is released after more than five years in prison.

In September 1998, the minister of justice decided to release Clayton Johnson. Johnson walked out of jail after five years behind bars.

Four months later, Canadian officials dug up his wife's body. Dr. Linda Norton flew to Nova Scotia. She and a team of pathologists performed a second autopsy on Janice Johnson. For four days, they worked on the body. They found a **fracture** at the base of the **skull** that was probably produced by a backward fall. "We were able to see that the base of the skull was lifted up about a half an inch," says Norton.

Almost ten years after her death, Janice Johnson's body was dug up for a second autopsy. Experts agreed that the skull fracture could have been caused by a backward fall down the stairs.

By the end of the autopsy, the team members released their findings. Janice Johnson probably died accidentally after falling backward down her basement stairs.

In February 2002, the Canadian government dropped the charges against Johnson. Thirteen years after his wife's death, Clayton Johnson had finally been cleared.

Johnson got a public apology from the Canadian government. He was also awarded more than two million dollars.

Johnson has forensic science to thank for his freedom. Otherwise, says Dr. Norton, he "would still be sitting in jail accused of a crime that did not even occur."

Instead, Clayton Johnson is living near his daughters in Nova Scotia. He spends time with his grandchildren and thinks about his wife often. He still sees some of the jurors who found him guilty. They don't talk about the case at all, he says. 24/7

Clayton Johnson leaves the courthouse with his daughters in September 1998. He had served five years of a life sentence. It had been almost ten years since his wife, Janice, had died.

FORENSIC

DOWNLOAD

Examine this! Here's even more amazing stuff about forensic pathology.

IN THIS SECTION:

▶ modern forensics in ANCIENT CHINA;

▶ tools of the trade for EXAMINING DEAD BODIES;

▶ a quiz to see if you should be DISSECTING CORPSES for a living.

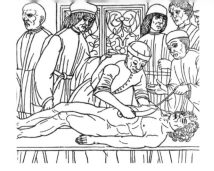

1248 Wash It Away

In China, a book explains how to use medical knowledge to solve crimes. The book is called *The Washing Away of Wrongs*. It describes types of wounds. It also tells how to distinguish between natural deaths and murders.

1530 Docs in Charge

Emperor Charles V of England orders that a medical doctor must determine the cause of unnatural deaths. Before 1530, coroners—who had no medical background—were in charge of investigating deaths. *Above:* An autopsy in about 1493.

Key Dates in Forensic

1813 Drug Test

Spanish doctor Mathieu Orfila develops the first toxicology tests. He explains that tissue samples should be taken during autopsies. The samples should be tested for poisons. At the time, poisoning was the leading cause of death in murder cases.

1915 Twice Dead

New York City hires a medical examiner to investigate deaths. Before 1915, all deaths were investigated by a coroner. The coroner was paid for each body he reported. Investigators found that he took advantage of the system. He left bodies where they would be rediscovered. When a corpse was brought in for the second time, he collected a second fee. *Left:* A morgue in New York City in 1890.

1807 Crime-Fighting School

The University of Edinburgh, in Scotland, opens the first forensic science program. The program has a professor of legal medicine.

Early 1600s
Early Autopsy

Two Italians, Fortunato Fidelis and Pado Zacchia, begin performing autopsies. They write reports that explain their work. The reports describe bullet and stab wounds. They also describe deaths caused by strangulation. *Right:* An autopsy in about 1666.

Pathology

Forensic pathology might be new to you, but it's been around for hundreds of years.

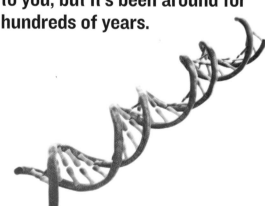

1985
Gene Pool

Sir Alec Jeffreys develops **DNA** testing. DNA tests help doctors identify victims. They can also prove a suspect's guilt or innocence. Forensic pathologists are now more careful than ever to preserve bodies just the way they are found.

Forensic pathology is front-page news.

"Dr. Death" Helps Tidal Wave Victims

PHANGNGA PROVINCE, THAILAND—January 13, 2005.

In December 2004, a deadly **tsunami** swept through the Pacific Ocean. The wave hit Thailand hard. It left more than 5,000 people dead.

Each one of these bodies had to be identified. That job fell to Khunying Porntip Rojanasunan. As the *New York Times* reports, she's known in Thailand as Dr. Death. She oversees dozens of autopsies here every day.

Dr. Porntip does not look like a typical Thai doctor. She dyes her spiked hair purplish red. She wears jeans and an ear cuff. She says she chose forensics because she did not fit in as an ordinary doctor. "I work with the dead," she says, "and the dead do not complain."

Dr. Khunying Porntip Rojanasunan is the best-known forensic pathologist in Thailand. She helped identify bodies after a devastating tsunami hit her country in December 2004.

Autopsy Shows Policeman Died From 9/11 Dust

OCEAN COUNTY, NEW JERSEY—April 12, 2006

James Zadroga spent 470 hours working at the ruins of the World Trade Center after September 11, 2001. Zadroga was a detective with the New York City police. He died in January of **respiratory failure**. (That means he couldn't breathe.)

The Ocean County coroner said today that Zadroga died from dust he breathed in at Ground Zero. A clinical autopsy showed dust in his lungs. It also revealed damage to his liver, heart, and spleen. The report is the first proof that work at the World Trade Center site may have caused **fatal** damage.

New York City police detective James Zadroga worked for hundreds of hours at the World Trade Center site (*above*). This work may have exposed his body to deadly dust. He died in January 2006. *Left:* James Zadroga's funeral.

Autopsy 101

When there's a suspicious death, pathologists perform a forensic autopsy. Here are some of the steps they take.

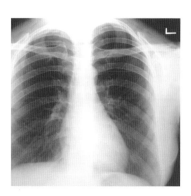

Documenting the Corpse

All bodies are weighed and measured when they come into the morgue. Usually, they are fingerprinted, too. Most morgues photograph the body both clothed and unclothed. Sometimes, the body is **x-rayed**. The **corpse**'s hair and eye color are noted, as well as scars, tattoos, and other marks.

Examining the Clothes

The forensic pathologist examines the clothes for any **trace evidence**, such as hairs, fibers, and blood. She also looks for holes on the clothing that could have been caused by weapons.

Examining the Corpse

The pathologist then carefully removes the clothing. She begins to examine the outside and inside of the victim.

External: The pathologist continues to look for trace evidence. For example, she checks for skin under the fingernails. She also notes signs of violence, such as knife and bullet wounds. (See page 10.)

Internal/Torso: The pathologist then opens up the corpse's **torso**. That's the part of the body above the waist. She makes a Y-shaped incision, or cut, from shoulder to shoulder. Then she cuts down to the pubic area. That allows her to remove and examine the heart, lungs, and other organs. She also collects samples from the stomach.

TIME OF DEATH

Forensic pathologists look for three clues that can help them figure out how long a body has been dead.

Algor mortis has to do with body temperature. Body temperature decreases about one degree every hour after a person dies.

Livor mortis has to do with the settling of blood in the body. After death, blood cells collect at the lowest point in the body. The position of the cells suggests what position a person was in at death.

Rigor mortis has to do with the stiffening of the body after death. About two hours after death, the face muscles become stiff. Twelve hours after death, the entire body becomes rigid. Then the body begins to loosen up. Thirty-six hours after death, the body feels soft again.

Internal/Brain: The pathologist then opens the skull. She makes an incision over the top of the head, from ear to ear. She then peels the scalp forward. She uses a saw to cut away part of the skull. She examines the brain in the skull. Then she removes it and examines it more closely.

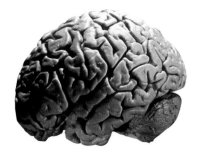

Returning the Organs

When the pathologist is finished, she returns the organs to the body. She sews up the corpse.

Autopsy Tool Box

Have a look at the tools, equipment, forms, and other stuff used by a forensic pathologist.

TOOLS AND EQUIPMENT

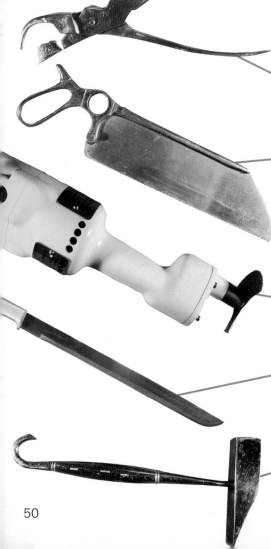

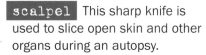

scalpel This sharp knife is used to slice open skin and other organs during an autopsy.

rib cutter To get to the heart and lungs, a pathologist has to remove the ribs. For that, she uses a rib cutter.

bone saw Bone saws are used to cut through human bones.

skull chisel This tool is similar to a sculptor's chisel. It's used to separate the skull bone from the brain.

vibrating saw The human brain is protected by a thick skull. To cut through it requires a vibrating saw.

knife Large knives with rough edges are used to cut slices of organs. Forensic pathologists often examine the slices under a microscope.

hammer with hook This tool pulls the skull off the body to reveal the brain.

scissors Sharp scissors are used to cut through skin, blood vessels, and soft organs.

enteretome Pathologists need a special kind of scissors to cut through the intestine.

hagedorn needle A hagedorn needle is used to sew up the body after the autopsy.

staple gun Sometimes a staple gun is used to close incisions after the autopsy.

face shield Forensic pathologists wear face shields to protect their eyes from blood and pieces of bone. This shield also helps to protect doctors from disease.

scrub suits Forensic pathologists wear the same uniform as doctors and nurses in the operating room.

latex gloves Latex gloves protect the hands during the autopsy.

BODIES OF EVIDENCE

Forensic pathologists take careful notes as they perform autopsies.

Forensic pathologists use these diagrams when writing up an autopsy report. First they note anything they've found on the body—bruises, burns, cuts, etc. A key at the bottom identifies the markings. They also write notes to themselves. Next, they note anything found inside the body. These findings are written up later in the autopsy report.

HELP WANTED:
Forensic
Pathologist

Dr. Norton is a forensic pathologist in private practice. She lives in Dallas, Texas.

How would you like to cut into the job of a forensic pathologist? Here's more information about the field.

Q&A: DR. LINDA NORTON

24/7: How did you get started as a forensic pathologist?

DR. LINDA NORTON: Well, I went to medical school. Then I became interested in forensic pathology. I started out at the Chief Medical Examiner's Office in North Carolina. I did most of my training at Duke University. Over 80 percent of what we did were homicides. Then, four months into my training, a DC-9 airplane crashed, so my focus shifted.

24/7: How do you put all the pieces together when you're trying to figure out the manner and cause of death?

NORTON: One of the lessons I've learned is that you can never have too much information. In fact, my daughters have been my "victims" on many occasions. I once had my oldest daughter lie in the tub in the same position a victim was in when she was found. I wanted to figure out how this young girl drowned.

24/7: What would you tell young people interested in forensic pathology?

NORTON: We desperately need bright young minds coming into this field. This really is a fascinating field. You get used to the grosser aspects. You become the only one who can make anything out of this kind of evidence.

24/7: What kind of training do you need to become a forensic pathologist?

NORTON: First, you have to be pre-med in college. Then you need to specialize in pathology for one year. Then you do a five-year residency program. You're 30 when you end up with your first real job. But you can be 30 and have a job that you just love, or a job where you're not as challenged. It's an exciting profession.

24/7: What part of your work do you enjoy the most?

NORTON: "Putting together the puzzle" is both fascinating and rewarding.

24/7: What do you like the least?

NORTON: Well, you do carry the odor. It gets into your hair.

THE STATS

DAY JOB
Besides working for states, cities, and counties, forensic pathologists can also work for medical schools, the military, and even the federal government.

MONEY
Average yearly salary for a forensic pathologist in the U.S.: $80,000 to $120,000

EDUCATION
Forensic pathologists must finish the following.
▶ 4 years of college
▶ 4 years of medical school
▶ 4–5 years in a residency training program in general pathology
▶ 1–2 years in a specialty training program in forensic pathology at a medical examiner's or coroner's office

DO YOU HAVE WHAT IT TAKES?

Take this totally unscientific quiz to find out if forensic pathology might be a good career for you.

1 Are you interested in science and anatomy?
a) I read everything I can about the human body.
b) I think it's sort of interesting.
c) I'm mostly interested in my next meal.

2 Are you good at communicating with people?
a) I'm great at talking with and explaining things to people.
b) Sometimes, but I can be shy, too.
c) No, I get frustrated when I have to explain things all the time.

3 Are you curious when you go to the doctor?
a) Yes, I ask a lot of questions.
b) Sometimes, but the explanations are kind of boring.
c) No, I just want to know how to stay healthy, so I don't have to go back.

4 Do you get grossed out easily?
a) No, in fact I like to watch operations on TV.
b) I don't mind the sight of blood.
c) I feel sick just thinking about that question.

5 Are you looking forward to college?
a) Yes, I've always thought I would get a graduate degree.
b) Yes, but I'm not that crazy about schoolwork.
c) I just want to get a job after high school.

YOUR SCORE

Give yourself 3 points for every "a" you chose. Give yourself 2 points for every "b" you chose. Give yourself 1 point for every "c" you chose.

If you got **13–15 points**, you'd probably be a good forensic pathologist.

If you got **10–12 points**, you might be a good forensic pathologist.

If you got **5–9 points**, you might want to look at another career!

HOW TO GET STARTED ... NOW!

It's never too early to start working toward your goals.

GET AN EDUCATION

- Focus on your science classes; take as many as you can. But don't forget English classes. You need to be able to write clear, correct reports.

- Start thinking about college. Look for schools with good pre-med programs.

- Read the newspaper. Keep up on what's going on in your community.

- Read anything you can find about autopsies and forensic pathology. See the books and Web sites in the Resources section on pages 56–58.

- Participate in speech-related activities like debate. Forensic pathologists are called on to speak in court and in the media.

- Graduate from high school!

NETWORK!

- Find out about forensic groups in your area.

- Call your local law enforcement agency. Ask for the public affairs office. Find out if you can interview a forensic pathologist or medical examiner about his or her job.

GET AN INTERNSHIP

Get an internship with a law enforcement agency or a local lab—in a morgue, if possible.

LEARN ABOUT OTHER JOBS IN THE FIELD

There are forensic labs in many police departments and sheriff's offices. You can also find out about working in the medical examiner's office. Or try one of these U.S. agencies: Drug Enforcement Administration (DEA); Bureau of Alcohol, Tobacco, Firearms and Explosives (ATF); Federal Bureau of Investigation (FBI); United States Postal Service (USPS); Secret Service (SS); Central Intelligence Agency (CIA); the military forces; the United States Fish and Wildlife Services (FWS).

FORENSIC DOWNLOAD

CAREERS

Resources

Looking for more information about forensic pathology? Here are some resources you don't want to miss!

PROFESSIONAL ORGANIZATIONS

American Academy of Forensic Sciences (AAFS)
www.aafs.org
410 North 21st Street
Colorado Springs, CO 80904-2798
PHONE: 719-636-1100
FAX: 719-636-1993

The AAFS is an organization for forensic scientists. It helps them meet and share information with other forensic experts. Its Web site includes a long list of colleges and universities with forensic science programs.

National Association of Medical Examiners (NAME)
www.thename.org
430 Pryor Street SW
Atlanta, GA 30312
PHONE: 404-730-4781
FAX: 404-730-4420
E-MAIL: Denise.McNally@thename.org

NAME stands for the National Association of Medical Examiners. It helps medical examiners learn and communicate with one another. The Web site includes recently published research, tutorials, and even job information.

Armed Forces Institute of Pathology (AFIP)
www.afip.org
6825 16th Street NW
Washington, DC 20306-6000
PHONE: 202-782-2100
E-MAIL: owner@afip.osd.mil

The AFIP is an agency of the Department of Defense that specializes in pathology consultation, education, and research. This group shares information with people around the world. The Web site has everything from published articles to information about upcoming classes.

WEB SITES

Disaster Mortuary Operational Response Team (DMORT)
www.dmort.org
The Disaster Mortuary Operational Response Team is an organization that assists local authorities during large disasters. The Web site has information about regional team sites and even online training.

HBO's Autopsy
www.hbo.com/autopsy/index.html
This Web site is from the HBO show *Autopsy*, starring Dr. Michael Baden. It is a terrific resource. The site features real-life cases, videos, a forensic timeline, and an interactive autopsy.

Miami-Dade Medical Examiner's Office
www.miamidade.gov/medexam/ home.asp
The Miami-Dade Medical Examiner's Office offers detailed information about how the office works. It's a good site to visit if you want to get a feel for what it's like to work as a forensic pathologist.

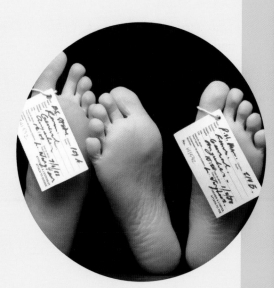

BOOKS ABOUT FORENSIC PATHOLOGY

Baden, Michael M., MD, with Judith Adler Hennessee. *Unnatural Death: Confessions of a Medical Examiner.* New York: Ballantine Books, 2005.

Baden, Michael M., MD, with Marion Roach. *Dead Reckoning: The New Science of Catching Killers.* New York: Simon & Schuster, 2002.

DiMaio, Vincent J., and Dominick DiMaio. *Forensic Pathology: Practical Aspects of Criminal and Forensic Investigations.* Boca Raton, Fla.: CRC Press, 2001.

Spitz, Dr. Werner U., and Daniel J. Spitz. *Spitz and Fischer's Medicolegal Investigation of Death: Guidelines for the Application of Pathology to Crime Investigation.* Springfield, Ill.: Charles C. Thomas, 2006.

BOOKS FOR YOUNG ADULTS ABOUT FORENSIC SCIENCE

Innes, Brian. *The Search for Forensic Evidence.* Milwaukee: Gareth Stevens, 2005.

Lane, Brian. *Eyewitness: Crime & Detection.* New York: Dorling Kindersley, 1998.

Platt, Richard. *Forensics.* Boston: Kingfisher, 2005.

Rainis, Kenneth G. *Crime-Solving Science Projects: Forensic Science Experiments.* Berkeley Heights, N.J.: Enslow Publishing, 2000.

Silverstein, Herma. *Threads of Evidence: Using Forensic Science to Solve Crimes.* New York: Henry Holt, 1996.

Walker, Pam, and Elaine Wood. *Crime Scene Investigations: Real-Life Labs for Grades 6–12.* New York: Jossey-Bass, 1998.

A

algor mortis (AL-gor MOR-tus) *noun* the dropping of the body's temperature after death

autopsy (AW-top-see) *noun* an internal and external examination of a dead body

C

clinical autopsy (KLIN-uh-kul AW-top-see) *noun* an autopsy done on someone who has died of natural causes

coroner (KOR-uh-ner) *noun* a government official appointed to investigate unnatural death; usually not a medical doctor

corpse (korps) *noun* a dead body

D

death certificate (deth ser-TIH-fuh-kut) *noun* an official record of someone's death

DNA (DEE-en-ay) *noun* a chemical found in almost every cell of your body. It's the blueprint for the way you look and function.

E

evidence (EV-uh-dunss) *noun* materials gathered in an investigation and used to prove someone's guilt or innocence

exhume (eg-ZOOM) *verb* to dig up a corpse from a grave

expert (EX-purt) *noun* someone who has special knowledge and experience in a given subject. See page 12 for a list of forensic experts.

F

fatal (FAY-tul) *adjective* deadly; having no cure

forensic autopsy (fuh-REN-zick AW-top-see) *noun* the examination of a body for evidence in a court case

forensic pathologist (fuh-REN-sick path-AHL-uh-just) *noun* a medical examiner; examines bodies in cases of violent, suspicious, or unnatural death

foul play (fowl play) *noun* an act of criminal violence

fracture (FRAK-shur) *noun* break; something that is broken or ruptured

Dictionary

H

hemorrhage (HEM-rij) *noun* a discharge of blood that results from broken blood vessels

homicide (HOM-uh-side) *noun* murder; the killing of one human being by another

J

jury (JU-ree) *noun* a group of people who listen to a court case and decide if someone is guilty or innocent

L

livor mortis (LIH-ver MOR-tus) *noun* the settling of blood in the body after death

M

ME (EM-ee) *noun* short for *medical examiner*

medical examiner (MED-uh-kul eg-ZAM-uh-nur) *noun* a doctor who directs the examination of bodies in murder cases and other suspicious deaths

morgue (morg) *noun* a place where dead bodies are kept. The bodies stay in the morgue until they are released for burial or cremation.

motive (MOH-tuv) *noun* a reason for doing something

P

pathologist (path-AHL-uh-just) *noun* a doctor who studies changes in the body's tissues and fluids that lead to disease

R

respiratory failure (RES-puh-ruh-TOR-ee FAYL-yur) *noun* a condition marked by the inability to breathe

rigor mortis (RIG-ur MOR-tus) *noun* the stiffening of the body after death

S

skull (skul) *noun* the bony structure that covers the head

spatter (SPAH-tur) *noun* the scatter and splash of drops of liquid (like blood)

suspect (SUS-pekt) *noun* someone who officials think may have committed a crime

T

torso (TOR-soh) *noun* the part of the body that's above the waist

toxicology (tok-sih-KOL-uh-gee) *noun* the study of drugs and poisons in the body

trace evidence (trays EV-uh-dunss) *noun* materials like tire tracks, dirt, and fibers that are left at a crime scene

tsunami (tsoo-NAH-mee) *noun* a very large, destructive wave caused by an underwater earthquake or volcano

V

victim (VIK-tum) *noun* a person who is injured, killed, or mistreated

X

x-ray (EX-ray) *verb* to photograph with radiation; x-rays help doctors see inside human body parts.

Index

agents, 12
algor mortis, 49
Ambien (sleep medication), 24,
    26–27
Association in Defense of the
    Wrongly Convicted (AIDWYC),
    37, 39
autopsies, 8, 11, 18, 19, 21, 23,
    28, 37, 38, 41, 44, 45,
    48–49, 51
Autopsy (TV show), 28

Baden, Michael, 28, *28*
blood, 10, 23, 24, 30, 34, 35–36,
    38, 40, 48, 49, 51
body temperature, 49
bone saws, 50, *50*
Bureau of Alcohol, Tobacco,
    Firearms and Explosives
    (ATF), 55

Campbell, Phil, 37–38, 38–39
Canadian minister of justice, 39, 41
cause of death, 11, 22, 24, 34,
    37, 52
Central Intelligence Agency (CIA), 55
Charles V, emperor of England, 44
clinical autopsies, 9
conclusions, 14, 38
coroners, 9, 18, 19, 21, 33, 34, 36,
    37, 44, 47

death certificates, 19, 34, 36, 37
detectives, 12
dieners, 12
DNA testing, 45
Drug Enforcement Administration
    (DEA), 55

education, 53, 55

enteretomes, 51, *51*
evidence, 9, 11, 12, 14, 22, 23, 25,
    26, 28, 37, 38, 39, 40, 48,
    51, 53
exhumation, 9

face shields, 51
Federal Bureau of Investigation
    (FBI), 28, 55
Fidelis, Fortunato, 45
Fillinger, Halbert, 18, 21, 22
food samples, 22, 24, 48
forensic autopsies, 9, 48
forensic nurses, 12
forensic pathologists, 9, 10, 11,
    12, 14, 19, 22, 25, 28, 36,
    38, 45, 48, 49, 50, 52–53
forensic toxicologists, 12
foul play, 9, 10

hagedorn needles, 51, *51*
hammers, 50, *50*
homicide, 8, 11, 24
Hood, Ian, 21–22, 23, 24
Hutton, Charles, 36

identification, 11, 45
internships, 55

Jeffreys, Sir Alec, 45
Johnson, Clayton, 30, *31*, 32, 33,
    34, 35, 36, 37–38, 41–42, *42*
Johnson, Janice, 30, 32, 33–34,
    36, 38, 40, 41

King, David, 36
knives, 50, *50*

Laboratory of Forensic Science, 38
latex gloves, 51, *51*
life insurance, 20–21, 25, 27, 35
Lockyer, James, 37–38, 38–39

MacDonell, Herb, 38–39, *39*,
    40, *40*
manner of death, 11, 22, 52

medical examiners (MEs), 8, 12, 19, 21–22, 23, 28, 37, 44
Merion, Pennsylvania, 16, *17*, 19
Molloy, Robert, 30, 32
morgues, 8, 12, *44*, 48, 55
motives, 35
Murphy, Heather, 39, 40, *40*

New York Times newspaper, 46
Norton, Linda, 38, 40, 41, 42, 52–53, *52*
notes, 51

Oldford, Brian, 35, 36
Orfila, Mathieu, 44

Perry, Roland, 33, 34, 36, 37, 38
Porntip Rojanasunan, Khunying, 46, *46*

questions, 11, 14, 22, 38
quiz, 54

Rabinowitz, Craig, 16, 18, *19*, 19–21, 24, 25, 26–27, *27*
Rabinowitz, Haley, 20, 25
Rabinowitz, Stefanie, 16, *16*, 18, 19, 20, 21, 22, 23, 24, 26, 27
residency training, 53
rib cutters, 50, *50*
rigor mortis, 49

salaries, 53
scalpels, 50
scissors, 51, *51*
scrub suits, 51
Secret Service, 55
September 11 attacks, 47
Shelburne, Nova Scotia, 30, *31*
skull chisels, 50
staple guns, 51, *51*
strangulation, 11, 23, 24, 26-27, 45

Thailand, 46
time of death, 11, 24, 49

toxicology tests, 22, 23, 24, 44
trace evidence, 48

United States Fish and Wildlife Services (FWS), 55
United States Postal Service (USPS), 55
University of Edinburgh, 45

vibrating saws, 50, *50*

The Washing Away of Wrongs (book), 44
Weybret, Tina, 35

Zacchia, Pado, 45
Zadroga, James, 47

Author's Note

There is no such thing as too much research. That's what Dr. Linda Norton told me. "You can never have too much information when you are doing an investigation," she explained.

True, we were talking about the Clayton Johnson case. But I think this applies to other things, too. As I wrote this book I was constantly coming across new information. Once I thought I understood something, I would learn something else that challenged my assumptions and pushed me to dig deeper.

That's the cool thing about research. You keep digging. You read as much as you can. You follow the path wherever it leads you. And you put the puzzle pieces together. I learned a lot writing this book. I hope you've learned a lot reading it—and that it makes you want to know even more.

ACKNOWLEDGMENTS

I would like to thank the following people for taking the time to talk about their work. Without their help, this book would not be possible.

Dr. Robert Middleberg, Director of National Medical Laboratories
Merv Stephens, Senior Crime Laboratory Analyst, Florida Department of Law
    Enforcement, Tallahassee, Florida
Ray Holbrook, Manatee County Sheriff's Office
Dr. Jan Garavaglia, Chief Medical Examiner for the District Nine (Orange-Osceola)
    Medical Examiner's Office in Orlando, Florida
Ellen Borakove, Office of the Chief Medical Examiner, New York City
Dr. John Hunsaker, President-elect, National Association of Medical Examiners
Dr. Linda Norton, Forensic Pathologist, Dallas, Texas
Winn Wahrer, Association in Defense of the Wrongly Convicted, Toronto,
    Ontario, Canada

CONTENT ADVISER:
H.W. "Rus" Ruslander, Forensic Supervisor, Palm Beach County (Florida) Medical
    Examiner's Office